Original title:
Petal Paintings

Copyright © 2025 Creative Arts Management OÜ
All rights reserved.

Author: Ronan Whitfield
ISBN HARDBACK: 978-1-80566-663-9
ISBN PAPERBACK: 978-1-80566-948-7

Whimsical Flora

Daisies in hats, they sway in glee,
Waving to bees, for a cup of tea.
Tulips in jeans, they laugh and play,
Wishing for sunshine to brighten their day.

Violets tell jokes while roses hum tunes,
Dancing with daisies beneath silver moons.
Petunias gossip in colors so bright,
Twinkling like stars in the warm, soft night.

Flourishing Narratives

Once a sunflower wore a crown,
Strutting around like a big, tough clown.
Lilies rolled dice, playing cards in the shade,
While ferns flipped burgers, the best ever made.

Snapdragons crack jokes, oh what silly sights,
As marigolds giggle in colorful tights.
Each bloom has a story, each leaf has a laugh,
In this garden of humor, let's take a big half!

A Kaleidoscope of Dreams

Hibiscus in flip-flops, beach vibes in tow,
Splashing in puddles, putting on a show.
Dandelions drift like confetti in air,
While clovers do cartwheels without any care.

Geraniums sing in a jazzy old tune,
Dancing on rooftops beneath a bright moon.
Each color a giggle, each scent a delight,
In this playful garden, where laughter takes flight.

Nature's Sketchbook

Sketches of laughter in shades of the day,
Pansies in scarves, they've got style on display.
Bumblebees buzzing like tiny composers,
While poppies paint murals on windswept disposers.

Cacti in sunglasses, oh what a sight!
Grinning through spines, giving friends quite a fright.
Every flower captured, each leaf with a grin,
In this sketchbook of nature, let's dance and spin!

The Vibrance Beneath

In gardens where the colors clash,
A flower sneezed, oh what a splash!
"Excuse me!" it laughed, with pollen proud,
As daisies giggled, a merry crowd.

The tulips danced in bright array,
Waving hello in a breezy way.
A bee flew by, quite lost in bliss,
Mistaking a rose for a giant kiss!

Silhouettes of Spring

The daisies wore their skirts so fine,
With laughing bees that zoomed in line.
A butterfly, with flair to show,
Said, "I'm the fashionista of the row!"

The sun winks down, a golden glee,
While flowers whisper, "Look at me!"
A gopher popped out, looking around,
"Oh dear, I thought this was underground!"

Brushstrokes of Emotion

The violets painted in shades of blue,
Swirled with joy, like morning dew.
"I'm happier than a pie on a plate!"
Cried a sunflower, "Isn't it great?"

The lilies blushed in bold red light,
Wobbling around to feel just right.
A hummingbird flaunted its tiny flair,
"Catch me if you dare, if you dare!"

The Colors of Awakening

Awakening with laughter in the air,
The flowers giggle without a care.
A rogue daffodil played peek-a-boo,
While a snail slid by—what a view!

The sunbeam tickled the ferny floor,
"Come out and play," it called for more.
A ladybug grinned, "Let's start a race!"
And all of them dashed, in happy pace!

Illuminations of Nature's Essence

In gardens bright, where colors clash,
The flowers gossip, with quite a splash.
They tell tall tales, of bees in flight,
And how they're dressed up, just for tonight.

With petals like skirts, they twirl and sway,
In a sunny dance, they laugh and play.
Each bloom a joker, with pollen dust,
In nature's circus, they're a must!

Mosaic of Garden Secrets

Hidden treasures in every bloom,
A daisy's wink, dispels the gloom.
Roses laugh in their velvet wear,
While tulips gossip without a care.

The daisies chuckle, the lilies tease,
While bumblebees do as they please.
In this mosaic, secrets intertwine,
Nature's humor is truly divine!

Harmonizing Hues Across the Field

Across the field where colors sing,
A purple giggle and a yellow fling.
The sunflowers grin at the clouds above,
Lending their cheer, twirling in love.

The poppies skip in their scarlet dress,
As daisies mime a clumsy mess.
A riot of colors, a joyful spree,
Nature's jester, wild and free!

Tints of Serenity in Floral Realms

In quiet corners, blooms convene,
Whispering secrets, like in a dream.
Violets giggle in soft pastel,
While the roses blush, under a spell.

A whimsical breeze brings laughter near,
As daisies say, 'We've nothing to fear!'
In this serene, yet lively show,
The garden winks, stealing the glow!

Caress of Color in Gentle Breezes

In gardens where laughter blooms,
Daffodils dance to sunny tunes.
Butterflies giggle, wings a-flutter,
While bees hum sweet, sticky butter.

Colors collide in a vibrant spree,
A riot of shades, wild and free.
Tulips tease with their flamboyant flair,
While daisies drop jokes, oh, beware!

Winds whisper silly secrets untold,
Petals form stories, bright and bold.
Each flower snickers in fragrant delight,
Painting the day from morning to night.

Nature's cabaret, a whimsical show,
Where colors swirl, and giggles flow.
In this canvas, joy takes its flight,
With every stroke, the world's bright light.

The Intricate Weaves of Flora and Time.

In the tapestry of blossoms, thoughts combine,
Dandelions gossip, their heads all align.
Roses wear crowns, with thorns as their jokes,
While sunflowers nod with a smirk like folks.

Time tickles petals on every breeze,
As violets chuckle, shaking their leaves.
Lilies prance proudly, while poking fun,
At busy bees buzzing, up to no good run.

Clovers pull pranks, their luck to promote,
While marigolds jiggle in hues to gloat.
Time paints each moment with playful grace,
In the garden where laughter takes its place.

Weaving bright tales, flora's fun spree,
With colors and whispers, blending with glee.
Each bloom a character, unique in the show,
Nature's great story, with joy on the go!

Whispers of Color

Colors chat softly in the sun's warm glow,
Petunias laugh, putting on quite the show.
Pansies wink under their vibrant hats,
As butterflies giggle, avoiding the cats.

Morning glories yawn, stretching out wide,
While tulips exchange jokes, in petals they hide.
Dew drops sparkle, bearing secrets of dreams,
Among blooms that chatter in bright sunshine beams.

Each flower's a jester, right in their place,
With jokes that they'd share if given a space.
Orchids flirt lightly with breezes just so,
Unraveling laughs in a colorful flow.

A garden of humor, a riotous sight,
Where colors converse 'til the fall of the night.
Nature's own theater, in hues so divine,
Whispers of laughter, where sunlight does shine.

Nature's Brushstrokes

In the canvas of life, colors collide,
Sunshine and rainbows take joy in their ride.
Silly daffodils doodle with flair,
While roses hold brushes, painting the air.

Tulips tiptoe as they waltz with the breeze,
With giggles and grins, they sway with such ease.
Lilies whisper secrets, oh, what will they say?
As daisies rejoice in a light-hearted play.

Nature's artistry, clumsy yet bold,
Brushstrokes of laughter, a sight to behold.
Each hue tells a tale, quirky and bright,
Creating a masterpiece, pure delight.

With every stroke, the laughter we gain,
In this vibrant world, joy dances, not vain.
Colors come alive in this playful embrace,
Nature's own laughter, a beautiful space.

Spectrum of Serenity

In gardens bright, like a toddler's dream,
Colors splashed with an artistic theme.
Bees buzz like they're in a rap battle,
While flowers giggle in their floral saddle.

Sunshine smirks, painting shadows with glee,
A squirrel steals snacks, full of esprit.
Butterflies dance in a dizzying loop,
As if trying to start a butterfly troupe.

The wind whispers secrets, tickles the dandelions,
While daisies nod like they're part of the Pantheon.
Hearty laughter sprinkles through the trees,
As petals argue over who sways with ease.

A snail eye-rolls, just moves slow for the show,
In this wacky realm where the blossoms all glow.
Laughing blooms make each critter confess,
Life's just a jest, dressed in floral finesse.

Blooming Inspiration

In a world where colors take a bold leap,
Tulips in tutus, throwing a party so deep.
Sunflowers flap like they're keen on the dance,
As hydrangeas laugh at the ladybug's prance.

Violets gossip, "Did you see that bee?"
With petals aflutter, they giggle with glee.
The roses roll over, mocking the hibiscus,
Making a ruckus, oh what a circus!

Daffodils twirl, just to steal the show,
While geraniums lecture on how to grow slow.
A daisy's sarcastic, "Look at my pose!"
As pansies declare, "We're the stars of the shows!"

And when the sun dips, it's a floral affair,
With nighttime blooms settling into their chair.
Petals still chuckle and spirits all soar,
As blooming inspiration opens wide every door.

The Language of Blossoms

In a meadow where the jokes bloom wide,
Roses whisper gossip they just can't hide.
Lilies stand proud, thinking they're so grand,
While marigolds mock, waving their little hand.

"Hey, did you hear?" says a zinnia in pink,
"The tulips are plotting! What do you think?"
A foxglove replies, "They think they are slick,
But I heard them trip, oh, that was the kick!"

Garden gnomes chuckle, holding their breath,
As flowers exchange quips until one's out of meth.
With swaying stems, they share a good laugh,
Making the insects all dance on their path.

The cosmos giggle with twinkling delight,
As night falls softly, dimming the light.
These blossoms converse in a language so sweet,
With punchlines and puns, nature's own heartbeat.

Dances in the Breeze

Watch the daisies jiggle in open air,
Their moves so goofy, you can't help but stare.
The violets waltz, thinking they're so slick,
While lilacs spin round, oh what a trick!

Breezy giggles and fluttering frays,
As blossoms sway in a dainty ballet.
Forget the formal—they just want to prance,
And insects are clapping, joining the dance!

In the soft whispers of soft morning rays,
Children of nature engage in their plays.
Hilarious petals, with stories to share,
Turn simple swings into flowing affair.

With pollen to sprinkle, they spread cheer anew,
As laughter bursts out in colors and hue.
In the wondrous waltz, joy takes its chance,
And life's quirky rhythm can't help but enhance.

The Spectrum of Sunlit Blooms

In a garden full of hues, so bright,
A flower wore a hat, what a sight!
With polka dots and stripes to wear,
It danced around without a care.

A daisy tried to do a flip,
But tripped and spilled its pollen drip.
The roses laughed, their thorns on show,
While tulips waved to steal the show.

Petals whispering in the breeze,
Telling jokes like swaying trees.
Sunbeams laugh, they play along,
In this garden, we all belong.

In a patchwork quilt of bloom and cheer,
The blooms create a fancy sphere.
Each color shouts, "Come join the fun!"
Life's a painting in the sun!

Strokes of Life in Petal Form

A violet tried to brush its hair,
With daffodils beside, debonair.
"You look like you caught a springtime cold!"
Narcissus teased, being quite bold.

Carnations tried a waltz so grand,
But stumbled on their own petal land.
With petals swaying, they lost the beat,
While bees buzzed round for a sweet treat.

A sunflower got a giant crown,
"I'm the king!" it said with a frown.
Tulips giggled, "You're just so tall,
We're the stars of this floral ball!"

Painting joy with every bloom,
In this garden, there's no gloom.
Each vibrant shade, a silly spark,
In the laughter of the park!

Dreamscapes in Floral Tints

A dreamer rests on petals soft,
While daisies giggle, oh, how they scoff!
"Wake up, sleepyhead! Time to play!"
They play hide and seek the day away.

A poppy said, "Let's start a band!"
With busy bees to lend a hand.
"Buzz, buzz, strum, and shake!" they sang,
A playful tune that made hearts hang.

Oh, but then the breeze blew by,
Twirling petals up to the sky.
Laughter echoed as they swirled,
In this vibrant, floral world!

Butterflies join in the fun and cheer,
With wings like laughter, bright and clear.
In pastel dreams, we find our glee,
An artful dance in nature spree!

The Aesthetic of Nature's Confetti

In a wild parade of color and glee,
Every flower plays dress-up, oh so free!
With zebras in stripes and polka-dot hues,
They throw a bash, it's a floral muse!

Lily tried to juggle, oh what a mess!
With smiling daisies in a floral dress.
They laughed so hard, the petals flew,
A sprinkle of pink and a dash of blue.

Lilacs twirled, a pirouette grand,
A petal explosion, like fireworks planned!
The tulips shouted, "Let's paint the sky!"
With every bloom, they waved hello, bye!

In this confetti of nature's delight,
Every color shines, oh what a sight!
Sprinkling happiness, everywhere spread,
In this wild garden, no room for dread!

Paint the Sky with Blossoms

A flower fell and hit my head,
I thought it was a bird instead.
It squawked and then it danced around,
A floral party to be found!

Bumblebees hum a merry tune,
While daisies sway and play the goon.
A tulip tried to jump in jest,
But tripped and fell in splendid jest!

The roses giggled, oh what fun,
As petals flew to greet the sun.
Each bloom a joke, a painted glee,
A garden full of comedy!

So grab your colors, let's not wait,
For nature's laughter at our gate.
With every brush, we'll light the way,
And bloom with joy, come what may!

Kaleidoscope of Nature

A butterfly in polka dots,
Was chased by squirrels, tied in knots.
The daisies giggled in delight,
As petals took off in a flight!

A sunflower lost its sense of sight,
And painted blue, it looked all right.
'Oh dear,' it said, 'what have I done?'
But all the colors had their fun!

The tulip wore a pair of shades,
And danced while others joined parades.
'Let's mix ourselves, my flowery friends!'
With all this laughter, joy transcends!

So swirl and twirl with every bloom,
We'll light up every room!
In this kaleidoscope we share,
Nature's humor everywhere!

Blooms of Imagination

In a garden full of dreams,
Mushrooms giggle by the streams.
A daisy dons a top hat grand,
And with a bow, it takes a stand!

A radish jokes about its shape,
Saying, 'I'm just a root escape!'
While violets tease the bumblebees,
In this wild, whimsical freeze!

The tulips sing a silly song,
While poppies sway, they sing along.
Each petal grins, a story told,
Imagination bright and bold!

Through every color, laughter sprinkles,
A burst of joy where sunshine twinkles.
So in this world of blooms and glee,
Let's wander where the wild hearts be!

Nature's Gift of Hue

The sun's a giant lemonade,
It spills on flowers, unafraid.
While giggling grasshoppers play,
In a vibrant, green ballet!

Roses wear confetti crowns,
While violets don silly frowns.
A clumsy bee trips on a bloom,
And lands right in a daisy's room!

The lilacs paint with joy divine,
In a swirling, wacky line.
Each hue a joke, a playful quirk,
Nature's laughter, how it works!

So let's embrace this colorful spree,
With every brush, let's be carefree.
In nature's gift of luminous cheer,
We'll spread the joy from year to year!

Nature's Color Chronicles

In a garden where colors collide,
The daisies wear shades of pride.
Roses giggle in dresses so bright,
While violets dance in pure delight.

Tulips with hats tipped to the sky,
Whispering secrets as butterflies fly.
Sunflowers bask in orange and gold,
Telling tales of the blossoms bold.

Dandelions puff up with a cheer,
Spreading wishes as they disappear.
Peonies blush in their fluffy attire,
While daffodils plot a prank in the mire.

Colors clash with a comic burst,
Nature's humor is always first.
A hue here, a chuckle there,
Laughter blossoms in fragrant air.

Vivid Moments

A bluebird sings with a wink and a hop,
As the tulips twirl and the daisies bop.
In this carnival of color and glee,
Even the hedgehogs dance with esprit!

Marigolds giggle in a sunny row,
While ferns shake it fast, putting on a show.
With every bloom, a chuckle's released,\nAs laughter
from petals never ceased.

Lilies sport stripes like a playful clown,
While lilies waddle in a colorful gown.
The insects join in the jovial spree,
Just buzzing along, oh so carefree!

Each moment's a splash of vibrant fun,
Where flowers frolic beneath the sun.
With laughter in leaves and colors astound,
Nature's comedy plays all around.

Garden Dreams in Hue

In the land where flowers all play hide and seek,
The poppies burst forth, they truly peak.
Daisies wear crowns, that's quite the sight,
While lilacs chuckle, feeling all bright.

Lavenders laugh in their sweet purple dreams,
They're plotting a prank, or so it seems!
Nasturtiums giggle as bees join the chat,
As they buzz around, oh, what's up with that?

A sunflower juggles their seeds with flair,
While clover makes wishes on a soft summer air.
Each bloom's a comedian, with petals aglow,
Creating a scene that's the best kind of show!

In this garden where colors conspire,
Giggles erupt as dreams dance higher.
True artistry blooms with each blooming chuckle,
In a vivid tableau, nature's bright buckle.

Living in Full Bloom

Life's a garden where plants like to tease,
With the tulips in shorts feeling breezy with ease.
Roses honk horns as they flirt and play,
While bumblebees buzz in a comedic ballet.

The orchids wear sunglasses, looking so cool,
While the daisies giggle at every pool.
In this vivid world where critters convene,
Even the worms have a sense of routine!

Petunias chat loudly in bright rainbow tones,
As the daisies swap stories with their jolly clones.
Each color a jest, each hue a quirk,
In this garden of laughter, nature's true work.

So come join the fun, let merriment loom,
In a sanctuary that's living in full bloom.
With humor and joy, the petals unfurl,
A colorful orchestra in a whimsical whirl.

Whispering Blossoms

Upon the breeze, they giggle bright,
Dancing in sun, oh what a sight.
With colors bold, they play their part,
They tickle noses, make hearts start.

A daisy wears a polka dot,
While tulips shout, "We're quite a lot!"
The roses blush, a playful tease,
While violets laugh, they sway with ease.

Bouncing petals in a line,
Tickling cheeks, oh how divine!
With every hue, they tell a joke,
In petals bright, their laughter woke.

Nature's Visual Poetry

A daffodil in sun lounged wide,
Said, "See my gold, I'm filled with pride!"
The poppies wink, they strut their stuff,
In fields of dreams, they can't get enough.

With every swirl and every spin,
Petals laugh, it's a goofy win!
Lavender whispers, "Scent me sweet,"
While daisies play hopscotch on the street.

They dress in colors, wacky style,
In nature's show, they go the extra mile.
With gusts of fun, they twirl and sway,
Petal giggles, all day play.

The Song of Blooming

In gardens wide, a chorus sings,
Harmony from tiny things.
The sunflowers grin, they dance in line,
Chanting, "We're tall and oh so fine!"

Lilies don bows, quite the affair,
While daisies jump, they shake their hair.
A symphony of colors bright,
In nature's band, they find delight.

The hummingbirds join in the tune,
Feeling groovy, morning to noon.
Together they laugh, as breezes flow,
With petals flapping, a blooming show.

Flourish of Color

With every hue, the blossoms jest,
In petals soft, they feel the best.
Marigolds shine, they flex and flex,
While lilacs giggle, "What's next?"

In fields of fun, they trip and roll,
Nature's art, it takes a toll.
The orchids pose in quirky ways,
In every bloom, humor plays.

Pansies wear hats, and poppies dance,
In vibrant shades, they take a chance.
With laughter loud, they spread a cheer,
In floral fun, there's nothing to fear.

Melodies of the Meadow

In a field of flowers bright,
A snail sings with all its might.
Bees are buzzing, lost in glee,
While ants dance like they're free.

Buttercups wear silly hats,
The daisies giggle at the chats.
Grasshoppers crack jokes, quite mad,
Nature's humor is a fad.

Sunflowers wave their golden heads,
While crickets jump on flower beds.
A caterpillar drops a rhyme,
Saying, 'Hey, let's waste some time!'

So come and romp in this great show,
Where nature's quirks are all aglow.
A meadow's dance, oh what a sight,
With laughter swirling, pure delight!

The Blooming Muse

A tulip whispers to a rose,
'Tell me, friend, how do you pose?'
The daisies laugh, they can't stay still,
While violets giggle, what a thrill!

Butterflies wear polka dot ties,
While bumblebees tell silly lies.
A ladybug's a fashion queen,
In spots of red, she reigns supreme!

The lilies twirl in jazzy beats,
While all the blooms share funny feats.
Each bloom a color, bright and stark,
In nature's play, it's quite the lark!

So tiptoe through this floral art,
Where every petal plays a part.
In blooms, a jest is always near,
A blooming muse, full of cheer!

Sun-kissed Strokes

With a brush of sunlight's gold,
The daisies boast, 'We're brave and bold!'
A sunflower winks, 'Can't you see?',
While tulips plead for comedy!

A painter parades through bright greens,
Humming tunes with delight teens.
The breeze giggles, sways the leaves,
As petals prank like little thieves!

Pansies laugh in shades galore,
While dandelions plot for more.
'We'll throw a party, small and sweet!'
With weed confetti, what a treat!

So come and join this playful spree,
With colors bright, so full of glee.
In sunlight's arms, with mirth we swim,
As nature simply loves to grin!

Nature's Reverie

In a garden, laughter peeks,
As tulips whisper quirky tweaks.
A bee says, 'Wait! I'm not done,'
While rosettes crack jokes for fun!

The wind joins in, it knows the score,
As petals swish and tease for more.
With playful sprigs and little quirks,
Each bloom does work to be a jerk!

Petunias boast of tales they spin,
Who knew that plants could grin and win?
With every color, vibrant themes,
Nature's laughter fills our dreams!

So sway with me in this delight,
Where flowers want to spark a fight.
In nature's realm, the humor flows,
A funny world where laughter grows!

Variegated Murmurs of the Earth

In the garden, flowers chatter,
They gossip on the day's bright matter.
A daisy winks at a dandelion,
While tulips plot to steal the show.

The roses blush with lover's tales,
As violets laugh with spinning jails.
Each petal flutters, a feathered cheer,
In this rumble of color, oh so dear.

Bees in bow ties buzz about,
With tiny hats, they jump and shout.
Frogs leap in joy, croak a joke,
While worms slide past in a thoughtful cloak.

Every bloom holds a secret grand,
Sharing tales in this vivid land.
With each petal toss, a sly wink sent,
Nature's humor, so well well-meant.

The Language of Blossoms Unfolded

A sunflower's smile beams so wide,
As petunias peek with giddy pride.
Laughter blooms in shades of green,
While daisies dream of places unseen.

The poppies blow bubbles of air,
As busy bees waltz without a care.
Lilies giggle beneath the sun,
And tulips tug at the breeze for fun.

In this garden, silliness reigns,
Where colors paint joy on windowpanes.
Petals whisper juicy tales,
Of mishaps and blooming fails.

With every stalk, a pun awaits,
As flowers tease at nature's fates.
The winds carry kites made of dreams,
As giggles ride on sunlit beams.

Canvas of Rain-Kissed Blooms

Raindrops dance on robust leaves,
While flowers spout gossip and cleaves.
A bashful rose hides from the rain,
Yet blossoms twirl with joy, unchained.

The daisies prance in puddles bright,
Splashing colors, pure delight.
A sunflower sticks out its tongue,
In a wet t-shirt contest, fun's begun.

Petals giggle as they drip and sway,
Each color brightens up the gray.
The jolly breeze sings funny songs,
As nature's laughter hums along.

Colors mingle, slip and slide,
In a joyful, splashy ride.
While clouds tiptoe in a fluffy line,
Whimsical wonders in nature's design.

Brush of Softness Beneath the Sky

Under the sky, the petals jest,
In this garden, humor's a guest.
With winks exchanged through the hue,
And chuckles shared, oh, what a view!

Breezes tickle the tender stems,
While blooms unite in silly gems.
A violets' dance in a swirling spin,
Teasing that spring will soon begin.

The sky laughs with a puffy smile,
As flowers proudly strut a mile.
With colors splashed like pies thrown high,
The laughter echoes, oh my, oh my!

Each day's brush paints a funny scene,
Where blossoms gossip, sweet and keen.
In this canvas of giggles and cheer,
Nature whispers softly in our ear.

Garden Symphony

In the garden, bugs take flight,
Bees wear tiny hats, what a sight!
Worms dance the tango, quite a show,
While daisies cheer with a gentle glow.

A squirrel conducts with a leafy stick,
While frogs croak tunes, it's quite a trick!
The roses laugh, their petals sway,
As ladybugs join the merry ballet.

Beneath the sun, the fun does grow,
Flowers gossip, putting on a glow.
With nature's sounds, such joy we find,
This garden's a stage for a rainbow grind!

So grab a seat, enjoy the view,
Nature's antics, so fresh and new!
In this funny show, let's join the cheer,
For every bloom, there's laughter near!

Colors of the Wind

Wind whispers jokes to the flowers bright,
Tulips giggle, what a delight!
Sunflowers turn, with grins so wide,
As breezes play tag, they run and slide.

Butterflies mimic, a silly dance,
Fluttering here, as if in a trance.
The violets tease, 'We're the best in blue!'
While pansies pout, 'Hey, what about you?'

Rainbows peek in where daisies bloom,
As passionflowers wiggle, making room.
The wind's a jester, full of glee,
Creating colors for all to see!

In this cheerful world of vibrant hue,
Laughter lingers, as the fun renews.
Let's paint our hearts with every breeze,
In this garden, we do as we please!

Impression of Spring

Spring arrives with a trumpet blast,
A giggly tulip says, 'What a blast!'
Daffodils applaud in sunny rows,
While bunnies hop in colorful clothes.

Chirping birds, with style so grand,
Wearing tiny shoes, they form a band.
The wind-tossed daisies start to sway,
Echoing laughter, a bright ballet!

Butterflies waltz on the air's embrace,
While bees' jokes buzz in each flower's face.
Lilies bounce, crowned with dew,
Stirring up giggles, just for you.

Spring's silly jesters make nature sing,
Creating laughter from everything.
Join the fun, let your worries fling,
In this joyful dance, feel the zing!

Secrets of the Sunlit Garden

In the sunlit garden, secrets unfold,
Where funny stories are often told.
Roses gossip, with whispers sweet,
While daisies dance on wobbly feet.

Behind the ferns, a rabbit peeks,
Making funny faces, no need for squeaks.
Caterpillars wear crowns made of leaves,
While ants plot pranks, oh, what a tease!

The sun spills laughter on every bloom,
Giggles resonate, dispelling gloom.
In this vibrant space, joy takes a stand,
With chuckles and fun, it's simply grand!

So wander through, find the playful spree,
These garden secrets for you and me.
With every bloom, a tale to tell,
In this sunlit wonder, we all dwell!

Whispers of Blossom Colors

In gardens where the daisies play,
A squirrel steals a bloom, hooray!
Butterflies wear fancy hats,
While bees buzz through like chubby acrobats.

The roses blush, they can't deny,
Why do sunflowers act so shy?
Lilies laugh with creamy grace,
As tulips pose in every place.

Jokes among the foliage spread,
A daffodil just lost its head.
With petals soft as cotton candy,
Even thorns can't seem too randy.

So come and join this floral romp,
Don't mind the ants that like to stomp.
In this jesting riot of hues,
Each bloom takes turns in silly shoes.

Canvas of Nature's Fragrance

A canvas stretched with scents so bold,
Where scents of jasmine never grow old.
Lemon zest from marigolds sings,
While dandelions dance on tiny wings.

Cactus wears a hat of snow,
While chubby bumblebees steal the show.
Chrysanthemums tease in soft pastels,
As fragrant gales ring like bells.

The violets whisper silly tales,
Of windblown spoons and fruity gales.
A floral band strums with delight,
As petals twirl into the night.

With laughter blowing through the trees,
And nature's brush drawing the breeze.
We paint the world in cheeky cheer,
As blossoms giggle, "Spring is here!"

Floral Hues in Morning Light

Morning dawns with hues that glow,
Like a rainbow got stuck in the snow.
Sunshine tickles the tulip-tips,
While giggling daisies do silly flips.

In the meadow, the blossoms conspire,
A thistle wearing a fancy attire.
Chortling pansies, quite the sight,
Have tea with asters, oh what a delight!

Frolicsome breezes tease the blooms,
With daffodils bursting like soft balloons.
Can you hear them sharing their dreams?
While honeybees plot in honey-sweet schemes.

Chasing shadows, the marigolds glee,
"Oh look, there's a gopher, come count with me!"
Each flower a prankster in morning's play,
As they bloom into mischief and sway!

Palette of the Soft Meadow

In the meadow of whims, colors collide,
Where daft daisies giggle, oh what a ride!
Buttercups dabbed in buttercream hues,
As grasshoppers sing their jazzy blues.

Every flower has a joke to share,
With lilacs who tease without any care.
"Why did the sunflower cross the street?"
"To show off its face, isn't that neat?"

Fluffy clouds take the audience's seat,
Gathering chuckles, oh what a treat!
Marigolds chuckling in the sun's warm glow,
Making mischief in the meadow below.

Each bloom a canvas, splashed in cheer,
Painting laughter with colors clear.
In this soft meadow of joy and jest,
Nature smiles, we are truly blessed.

The Dance of Floral Whispers

In gardens where the daisies prance,
The roses join in floral dance,
A daffodil trips on its stem,
While sunflowers grin, just let them!

Bees buzz around like tiny cars,
Pollinating under the stars,
Petals slip, like socks in clay,
Who knew flowers could be this gay?

The tulips twirl with all their might,
Waving at bees, oh what a sight!
While violets hide in laughter's glow,
They chuckle softly, "Let's steal the show!"

So next time you stroll through the bloom,
Just watch for giggles, the floral room,
For petals know how to make a scene,
In gardens, they're the funniest we've seen!

A Tapestry of Delicate Shades

In meadows bright, hues clash and blend,
Colors giggle, they twist and bend,
Crayons in bloom, with laughter so grand,
They scribble stories across the land.

Lavenders leap in lavender cheer,
While marigolds joke, "We're the brightest here!"
A clover sports a green bowtie,
With a wink like, "Watch me fly high!"

Pansies pout with purple grace,
They toss about the silliest face,
While chicory, oh so blue, it dreams,
Of playing jokes in daylight beams.

In this tapestry of color array,
Florals spin tales in a funny ballet,
Each shade a smile, a whimsical tale,
In every petal, laughter prevails!

Nature's Brush and Heartbeat

With each stroke of the morning sun,
Colors leap out, oh what fun!
Nature's brush paints all around,
In splatters of laughter, it's truly profound.

The daisies giggle, waving hello,
While hydrangeas blurt, "We're putting on a show!"
A sunflower teeters, its head held high,
With wishes to tickle the passing sky.

Each splash of color dances wild,
Like a playful and whimsical child,
The lilacs chime with a jolly tune,
As the crocus winks to the swooning moon.

So listen close to nature's art,
As giggles escape from every part,
With each bloom sharing its funny fate,
The world's a palette, so don't be late!

Echoes of Garden Charms

In the garden, a trumpet vine calls,
Echoes of laughter bounce off the walls,
With roses whispering secrets galore,
'What's the fuss? We bloom, we explore!'

The cosmos flaunt their cheeky grace,
"Catch us if you can, we're off to chase!"
While lilacs tickle with gentle glances,
Encouraging bees to join in the dances.

Zinnias giggle in full display,
"Who wore it best?" they joke and sway,
With petals blushing a vibrant hue,
Saying, "We're fabulous, how about you?"

So, wander through this charming scene,
Where flowers create the quirkiest glean,
In echoes of joy, they find their way,
Making gardens brighter every day!

Threads of Nature

In the garden, colors swirl,
Sticky fingers, watch them twirl.
Mixing hues, a silly spree,
Bees chuckle at our artistry.

Blossoms giggle in the sun,
Nature's canvas, pure fun.
Throw some green, splash on some blue,
What could possibly go askew?

Dancing leaves join the play,
While butterflies steal the day.
A mess of shades, a joyful fight,
Who knew dirt could bring such delight?

With every brush, a laugh takes flight,
A garden party, oh so bright.
Nature's artwork, wild and free,
Join the chaos, come and see!

Painted Memories

Hands in soil, we've gone astray,
Turns out mud's the price we pay.
Crayons lost, but who needs tools?
We'll just improvise like fools!

Petals plucked for a floral frame,
We giggle, forgetting the game.
A daisy here, a rose, why not?
Our masterpiece is quite a lot!

Oh look, a sunflower smile,
Flaunting hues in grand style.
Nature laughs as we create,
Memories bloom, it's all first-rate!

As colors blend, the sun dips low,
Our garden grows, a vibrant show.
With laughter shared, our hearts grow light,
Painted memories gleam so bright!

A Floral Odyssey

In fields where daisies dance and sway,
We craft our dreams in a playful way.
A brush mishap, the colors fly,
Who knew flower art would make us sigh?

Mixing shades with a cheeky grin,
Throw in a splash, let mischief begin!
Pollen fights and giggling bees,
Nature's laughter echoes through the trees.

A tangled vine becomes our throne,
Crowned with petals, we're overgrown!
Silly stories and silly stains,
In our journey, laughter reigns.

As the fragrance fills the air,
We dare to paint beyond compare.
A funny tale, of blooms and cheer,
An odyssey we hold so dear!

As the Flowers Speak

In the garden where flowers chat,
They gossip, giggle, and say, 'What's that?'
'Look at them, with paint on their nose!'
The blooms all shake, in joyful pose.

With splashes of color, they share a laugh,
'This won't end well,' says the autograph.
But we just chuckle and paint with glee,
What can go wrong? It's just a spree!

Wobbly strokes and plenty of cheer,
A sunflower whispers, 'No fear, my dear!'
As petals sway, they cheer us on,
A garden orchestra, from dusk till dawn.

Hummingbirds join the giggling train,
As we paint like children, taking their reign.
In nature's arms, our hearts take flight,
As flowers speak, we fill the night.

Hues of the Heart

A blue daisy danced on my head,
While green roses laughed as they fled.
The yellow sun teased the quiet ground,
As petals giggled round and round.

The purple blooms dressed up in style,
They strutted across with a cheeky smile.
Orange tulips playing hide and seek,
Whispering secrets, oh so unique.

The red poppies brewed some sweet tea,
While bees buzzed loudly, quite carefree.
Butterflies wore hats made of grass,
In this garden, fun times come to pass.

A flower broke into a bright jig,
Claiming it's the fairest, big or small, big!
With petals aplenty, we'll always play,
In this silly dance of the flowery ballet.

Nature's Palette

With a brush made of reeds, oh what a sight,
Paint splashes of colors, both day and night.
The daisies giggle, each one a clown,
While lilacs leap as they dance around.

Sunflowers wink at their neighbors near,
While violets whisper jokes, oh dear!
A clumsy insect trips on a leaf,
Triggers laughter, a comic relief.

The roses are scheming a grand parade,
With daisies leading, unafraid.
Tulips in tutus take to the stage,
Bringing cheer to this colorful page.

Every petal chuckles, every stem sways,
In this canvas wild, where chaos plays.
Nature's charades, in colors so loud,
A masterpiece made for the joyful crowd.

Echoes of Eden

In a garden warm, with colors so bright,
A tulip slipped in for a playful bite.
The lilies laughed, 'What a silly fed!'
As the daisies rolled down, quite misled.

Sunshine giggles as shadows swing,
While butterflies flap, oh what a fling!
The violets hum a catchy tune,
As chubby bumblebees buzz 'neath the moon.

A rose in a hat, what a sight to see,
Proclaims, "I'm the best, just watch me be!"
The daisies argue in a match of wits,
While petals tumble and throw little fits.

Echoes of laughter bounce from each leaf,
In this Eden of joy, there's no grief.
With colors aplenty, we romp and play,
In the laughter of blooms, we'll always stay.

Vibrant Wildflower Reverie

A bright daffodil wears a sun hat wide,
As purple asters take a bouncy ride.
The daisies spin pirouettes so grand,
While clovers clap, lending a hand.

Yellow blooms grinned, quite cheeky tonight,
Sprinkled confetti, oh what a sight!
With wildflowers dancing in a gleeful swirl,
The garden erupts as each blossom twirls.

Bees buzz in rhythm, a comical song,
While butterflies flutter along, so strong.
A zany marigold juggles a bee,
Declaring, "Watch me! I'm wild and free!"

In a vibrant dream where laughter resides,
With petals as friends, joy never hides.
The wildflower ball is a hilarious spree,
In the garden of giggles, come dance with me!

Life's Brush with Nature

In the garden, colors meet,
A clownish bee, skipping on feet.
Dandelions wear crowns like gold,
While shy violets remain bold.

A squirrel painted with a pine,
Jumps and giggles, oh so fine.
Butterflies in tutu swirl,
As the bumblebees give a twirl.

The Colorful Dance

Raindrops stomp on rainbow beams,
While flowers sway in silly dreams.
A daisy wears a polka dot,
While tulips spin, giving all they got.

The sun bursts in with a loud cheer,
As petals twirl without a fear.
Ladybugs join, their spots ablaze,
In this wacky, flowery craze!

Expressions of Flora

Oh, what a sight, the flowers grin,
Laughing petals, let the fun begin!
Honeysuckles tell jokes so sweet,
While roses dance with wiggly feet.

Chirpy crickets join the spree,
In a floral comedy, wild and free.
Pansies mock the butterflies,
As daffodils chuckle through the skies.

A Brush with Nature

A painter in a muddy coat,
Covers trees in jokes and hope.
He splatters colors here and there,
As squirrels watch with puzzled stare.

With each stroke, a giggle grows,
As mischief in a lily shows.
Nature's canvas, wild and bright,
Is filled with laughter, pure delight.

Brush of the Earth

With a swish and a swoosh, colors fly,
Grass stains my knees as I laugh and sigh.
Nature's brush tickles every stray leaf,
Turning the mundane into pure belief.

Dandelion fluff floats on a breeze,
Mixing with laughter, oh, such a tease!
I'll paint with my fingers, the sky so blue,
But my masterpiece looks like a zoo!

The flowers giggle, they know it's true,
Their vibrant hues are a madcap brew.
I dip my toes in puddles of cheer,
Creating chaos, but I have no fear.

So grab a brush, come dance in the green,
In this wild gallery, joy is the scene.
Nature's art calls us to take a chance,
Join me in this clumsy, colorful dance!

Palette of the Pure

A splash of yellow, a sprinkle of red,
Mixing up joy like it's all in my head.
Oh, what a mess! It's a party galore,
Every drop tells a tale, just beg for more.

I smeared some blue on my neighbor's cat,
He struts like a peacock; he's got style, just that!
With giggles and splatters, we paint the town,
Who knew such fun could turn us all brown?

Let's swirl and twirl with the colors we find,
Whimsical wonders, oh, the wittiest kind.
A critter parade with hues all around,
In this silly masterpiece, we're joyfully bound.

The sun starts to set, but oh, not too fast,
We'll paint the twilight, make memories last.
With brushes in hand, we'll conquer the night,
The palette of pure giggles is our delight!

Petals in Flight

Watch the blossoms take to the air,
Like tiny kites, they whirl without care.
Laughing and spinning, they dance in the sun,
Who knew such joy was so much fun?

A swarm of colors, a carnival fair,
Tickling the noses of all who dare.
Giggling daisies take over the scene,
With petals of laughter, they're bursting the seam.

They flutter and twirl, a whimsical spree,
I'm covered in pollen, so comically free!
Flying with flowers, I'm caught in the thrill,
This playful adventure could never stand still.

So come join me, let's create quite a sight,
As petals take flight, oh, what pure delight!
With each little chuckle, we'll brighten the day,
In this silly escapade, we'll giggle and play!

Canvas of Life

Life's a canvas, let's splash it with cheer,
Throw on some giggles, they're always near.
A stroke of mischief, a dab of surprise,
With colors of joy, let's paint up the skies.

Splattered with colors of every hue,
Silly shapes and lines all tell tales anew.
I tripped on a brush, now look at this mess,
An abstract of laughter, I must confess!

The world's our palette, let's mix it with zest,
Jokes in every corner, we're truly blessed.
As wild as the flowers that bloom in the field,
This canvas of life is a masterpiece revealed.

So grab your paint and let's make some noise,
In this colorful journey, we'll relish the joys.
With brushes in hand, we'll create with delight,
A funny little story that dances in light!

Brushstrokes of Springtime Dreams

In the garden of giggles, colors collide,
Bees in tuxedos dance side by side.
Sunflowers wear shades, feeling so cool,
While daisies do jokes, like wise little fools.

Rainbows tumble down, in puddles they play,
Wobbling worms sing, come join our ballet.
A splash of bright laughter, who could resist?
Nature's own canvas, an artist's delight twist.

The wind whispers secrets, tickles the grass,
With brushes of breezes, they all seem to pass.
Each flower a painter, with stories to tell,
In this funny ballet, do we do well?

So paint me a smile, let colors unwind,
In this whimsical world, leave dullness behind.
With each silly stroke, let laughter take flight,
As springtime awakens with colors so bright.

The Art of Fluttering Grace

Butterflies giggle, doing the cha-cha,
With silly antennae, how bizarre, ha-ha!
A family of blooms, all wearing a hat,
Doing the waltz with a chubby chitchat.

Grasshoppers juggle, while crickets chime in,
Twirling and swirling, let the fun begin.
Every color winks, while petals report,
It's a comical show, a nature court.

Dandelion puffs, with fluffy white dreams,
Blow a little kiss to the giggly streams.
The art of their movement, a sight so divine,
With a snicker and wink, let's share some sunshine.

So dance with the daisies, let laughter unfold,
In each fluttering grace, let stories be told.
Together we'll canvas the skies up so high,
With humor and color, let our spirits fly!

Wildflower Symphony on Canvas

A chorus of colors, in winds they declare,
Dancing on canvas, in laughter laid bare.
Wildflowers wiggle, serenading the bees,
Under a blue sky, with giggles and ease.

Breezes play trumpet, while daisies drum loud,
All of us gathered, a colorful crowd.
Petunias are painting, they splash with delight,
While tulips tell stories that tickle the night.

Swaying and laughing, a colorful spree,
With quips from the poppies, oh let's fill our tea!
Lilies in neon, made giant by cheer,
This symphony's sweet, let's all persevere.

So join in the chorus, make merry and bright,
This wildflower painting is pure laughter's light.
Together, we'll sway, with no care for the day,
Just a canvas of bloom, where fun finds a way!

Colors Born from Blooming Hearts

In a land of bright giggles, where flowers grow wide,
Colors burst forth, like joy we can't hide.
With blossoms like laughter, they twinkle and shine,
Each petal a secret, a silly design.

Roses wear socks, in shades of pink cheer,
While violets and tulips share every good spher.'
The daisies debate on who's funnier still,
In this garden of humor, our moods they fulfill.

The daffodils chuckle, as bees dance around,
Creating a ruckus, just look at them bound!
With every soft breeze, a giggle's expressed,
In vibrant reflections, we laugh and feel blessed.

So mix up the colors, let hearts intertwine,
In this bloom-filled oasis, our spirits align.
With laughter and love born from nature's own start,
We paint the world, colors born from each heart!

Aroma and Hue: An Ode to Bloom

A daisy wore a hat so grand,
With stripes and polka dots unplanned.
The tulips danced with all their might,
While roses giggled, oh what a sight!

Sunflowers tried a game of peek,
In shadows where the bumblebees sneak.
Each blossom burst in colors bright,
Chasing butterflies in pure delight!

Violets joined for the playful chase,
With humble bragging on their face.
The pansies laughed in shades of blue,
Making sure they each had their due.

As petals tumbled, swirling around,
They turned the garden upside down.
In this wild and joyful spree,
Nature's art made all hearts free!

Seasons Wrapped in Floral Masques

In spring, the flowers called for cheer,
With hats made of fruit, oh so dear.
A rose with sunglasses took a stroll,
While daisies played a lively role.

Summer's blooms wore flip-flops bright,
While violets basked in sunny light.
Each petal had a tale to tell,
In whispers soft, they rang the bell!

Autumn's blooms wore scarves of gold,
Gathering stories brave and bold.
Chrysanthemums tried to juggle leaves,
While laughing at the tricks up their sleeves.

Winter wrapped the flowers tight,
In coats of snow, a frosty sight.
Yet still they giggled, one and all,
Creating magic, a floral ball!

Vivid Echoes in the Twilight Garden

At twilight, blooms began to speak,
With petals bright and stems so sleek.
Lilies crack jokes about the moon,
While pansies hum a late-night tune.

Daffodils played hide and seek,
Promising a laugh every week.
With every breeze, the petals twirled,
Jazzing up their floral world!

As shadows danced and colors swayed,
The garden's mischief was well-laid.
Marigolds boasted of their flair,
While daisies winked without a care.

In twilight's arms, the blooms conspired,
Crafting laughter, never tired.
In nature's glow, their joy takes flight,
A silly show, a pure delight!

Harmonies of Nature's Paintbox

The garden holds a palette rare,
With colors splashed, floating in air.
Each flower strummed a note so fine,
Creating symphonies divine.

Sunflowers led a boisterous band,
While daisies played the tambourine stand.
Roses clapped, with petals so spry,
All flowers joined, reaching the sky.

In harmony, the colors sang,
As fireflies joined in the clang.
Laughter echoed through the night,
In nature's concert, pure delight!

With every bloom, a giggle grew,
Their joyous tunes, a bright debut.
As stars blinked down, the flowers swayed,
In perfect rhythm, they played!

Canvas of Blooms

On a canvas bright and wide,
Splatters of color glide,
Daisies wear polka dot pants,
While sunflowers do a dance!

With tulips doing the cha-cha,
And roses shouting 'No pas de deux!'
Bees caught in a comic spin,
Busy buzzing, they jump in!

Tapestry of Flora

On fabric stitched with flair,
Petunias pull style from thin air,
Lions wearing crowns of green,
Giggle as they preen and preen!

Geraniums sporting funky hats,
Garden gnomes chat with their cats,
A vine slips in, does a twirl,
Creating chaos in a whirl!

The Art of Blossom Dreams

In a gallery of bizarre sights,
Cacti wearing roller skates,
Orchids sneak a midnight snack,
Thieves dressed in leafy black.

The canvas drips with sticky paint,
While violets doodle, oh so quaint,
Sunsets mix with candy stripes,
Every flower sparks chucklingipes!

Floral Whirlwinds

In winds that twist and turn,
Petals swirl like moths that burn,
Bumbles riding their floral bikes,
Crashing into rosy spikes!

Hibiscus bring a pop and wink,
While lilies throw a bubble drink,
A dandelion wears a crown,
As all the colors tumble down!

www.ingramcontent.com/pod-product-compliance
Lightning Source LLC
Chambersburg PA
CBHW071828160426
43209CB00003B/244